EXAM ROOM 2
A one-act play

by

José Luis Hinojosa, MD

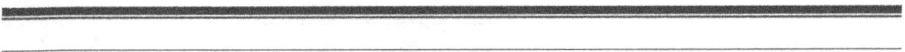

Also by José Luis Hinojosa, MD

NOVELS

The Tonic
Master and Disciple

PLAYS

Rosi Milagros
Chameleon

NONFICTION

The Language of Winners!
¡El Lenguaje de los Triunfadores!
Report Card on Rape
Magnets for Health
Tae Kwon Do for Everyone
Frozen in Time
The HELP Secret

SCREENPLAYS

Campeón (co-author)

Cast of Characters

MRS. LAWRENCE: Mrs. Wanda Lawrence is an elderly female patient who hurt her knee and is eager to get pain relief.

MR. LAWRENCE: Mr. Eric Lawrence is Wanda's husband.

JUAN SANCHEZ, MD: Dr. Sanchez is a fine family doctor with excellent reputation and training. He is also the boss at the clinic.

NURSE: Maggie is the nurse who escorts patients into the examination rooms and helps the doctor with their care.

RECEPTIONIST: The receptionist is that vital first impression at the clinic. She greets the patients and answers the phone. Okay, she's mainly on the phone.

CARLITOS: Carlitos is a little boy patient.

MOTHER: Carlitos' single mother.

FEMALE PATIENT: A young adult female patient.

PARAMEDIC: The ambulance worker who responds to the clinic's emergency.

Action

The action takes place in the medical clinic of Doctor Juan Sanchez in McAllen, Texas.

Time

The play takes place on a winter day in modern times.

Scene 1

As the curtain opens, we see the reception area of a doctor's office full of patients. Classical music is heard softly over the lobby's speakers.

An elderly couple, ERIC and WANDA LAWRENCE, enter. As he holds the door open for her, MRS. LAWRENCE walks in. She is in obvious pain, and is limping; she also has a cane. She's wearing a nice pant-suit and her hair is freshly-made up.

MR. LAWRENCE looks like a strong man for his age. He's wearing a golf shirt, shorts, and a baseball cap. He's also carrying a plastic grocery bag full of medicines.

She's argumentative and is getting after him, then she pokes him with the cane. He doesn't make any attempts at talking back to her. She continues to hit him.

The RECEPTIONIST is on the phone... on a personal call. She just finished taking a selfie.

RECEPTIONIST. Hold on a second. (*turns to the couple*) Can I help you?

MRS. LAWRENCE stops hitting MR. LAWRENCE and pushes him forward, toward the window.

MR. LAWRENCE. Ahhh... What kind of doctor's office is this?

RECEPTIONIST. This is a family practice office. (*gestures for him to wait and goes back to phone conversation*)

MRS. LAWRENCE. (*approaches the window*) Excuse me! Miss... (*Cont'd*)

The RECEPTIONIST remains on the phone.

MRS. LAWRENCE. (*Cont'd*) Miss!

RECEPTIONIST. (*rolls eyes and puts conversation on hold*) Can't you see I'm busy here?

MRS. LAWRENCE. Oh, I see. I see that your little phone call can wait... but *I* certainly can't!

RECEPTIONIST. (*rude*) What can I do for you?

MRS. LAWRENCE. You can answer one very simple question for me.

RECEPTIONIST. (*to audience*) I'll be the judge of that.

MRS. LAWRENCE. Does the doctor see "geriatrics?"

RECEPTIONIST. (*with attitude*) Well... this *is* a family practice office.

MRS. LAWRENCE. (*mocking*) You didn't answer my question.

RECEPTIONIST. And *you* didn't hear my answer.

MRS. LAWRENCE. I heard you, lady. My hearing aides are working just fine, thank you.

MR. LAWRENCE. What my wife wants to know is, can the doctor see us?

RECEPTIONIST. (*flirtatious with him*) You should'a said that from the very beginning, sugar. Please wait a sec. (*goes back to phone*) Listen, I'll call you later, okay? (*mumbles*) I've got some old geezers who don't want to leave me alone. Hey, don't forget to check out my post from five minutes ago... (*Cont'd*)

RECEPTIONIST. (*Cont'd*) (*listens*) Yeah, my new selfie. Okay, I love you too, baby. (*mouths a kiss and hangs up*)
Now, where were we? Oh yes, do you have an appointment?

MRS. LAWRENCE. If we had an appointment, we wouldn't be *asking* you now, would we?

MR. LAWRENCE. (*to wife*) Calm down, sweetie. I know you're hurting... I'll take care of this. (*turns to RECEPTIONIST*) What my wife's trying to say is... no, we don't have an appointment. We're new to the area, you see.

MRS. LAWRENCE. We're from Minnesota.

RECEPTIONIST. Oh, how nice! You're winter Texans!

MRS. LAWRENCE. (*to audience*) Is she calling us names?

MR. LAWRENCE. Miss, what did you just say?

RECEPTIONIST. Winter Texans. That's what we call you folks from up North.

MRS. LAWRENCE. Well, that's just not a *nice* thing to say.

RECEPTIONIST. No, it's not a *bad* thing. It's kind'a... a way of making you feel at home.

MRS. LAWRENCE. (*facetious*) Aw, how cute. A home away from home. Don't shit on us with your name-calling, lady. I'm a keen observer of the human condition, and to me, you're shittin' us.

RECEPTIONIST. No, ma'am. I'm serious. It's good o'le southern hospitality.

MR. LAWRENCE. Well, since you put it that way... I guess you could say we're a little bit like... (*hugs wife*) snow birds.

MRS. LAWRENCE. (*shrugs him off*) Did you say 'love birds?' (*turns up her hearing aids*) Damned hearing aids... never work when you need 'em.

MR. LAWRENCE. (*leans to the RECEPTIONIST and says in semi-whisper*) We're trying to get away from the sub-zero weather that we have in Minnesota this time of year. (*winks at her and turns to wife*)

RECEPTIONIST. (*to audience*) Sub-zero weather? I think he brought it with him. (*points to MRS. LAWRENCE*)

MRS. LAWRENCE. Were you flirting with her?

MR. LAWRENCE. Of course not, my little winter Texan sweetie pie.

RECEPTIONIST. Oh, that's so cute.

MRS. LAWRENCE. What was that? Who are you calling cute?

RECEPTIONIST. (*begins to explain, but decides against it; addresses MR. LAWRENCE*) Can you please write your name on our sign-in sheet? (*hands him a blank paper; MRS. LAWRENCE notices this*)

MRS. LAWRENCE. But this is just a blank piece of paper! (*glances at other patients*) Aren't any of those people registered?

RECEPTIONIST. Sure they are, but we ask you to sign-in like this because of a new federal regulation that has something to do with confidentiality.

MRS. LAWRENCE. (*hesitant*) Well... you know I only heard every other word you said. (*to audience*) She talks so fast.

RECEPTIONIST. (*grabs other papers on clipboard and hands to her; speaks slower*) Take a seat and fill out this information. (*to MR. LAWRENCE*) Bring it back to me when you're done, okay sugar?

MRS. LAWRENCE. (*hits him on shoulder as they go sit*) You *are* flirting with her!

RECEPTIONIST picks up phone and dials; resumes her personal conversation.

MR. LAWRENCE places bag of medicines on floor next to him and MRS. LAWRENCE gives him the papers to fill out. She checks out the magazine rack, picks out a magazine and sits. A FEMALE PATIENT, early twenties, looks at bag and talks to MR. LAWRENCE.

FEMALE PATIENT. Looks like you've got yourself an entire pharmacy in there, ey?

MR. LAWRENCE. (*smiles*) Yeah, and you know? Funny thing is that most of those are not even mine!

FEMALE PATIENT. I see. They're hers, right? (*points towards MRS. LAWRENCE*)

MR. LAWRENCE. Yes, but don't say it too loud.

MRS. LAWRENCE. Did you say something?

MR. LAWRENCE. Nothing, sweetie.

MRS. LAWRENCE asks another patient, the MOTHER of a boy, CARLITOS, about the doctor.

MRS. LAWRENCE. So, is the doctor any good?

MOTHER. Oh yes, he's the best!

MRS. LAWRENCE. Ha! He's either really good... (*looks around waiting room*) or he's really slow.

MOTHER. Oh no, he *is* really good. He delivered this beautiful package. (*Proudly points to her son, age 4, who's sitting quietly beside her.*)

MRS. LAWRENCE. Did you say, *delivered?*

MOTHER. Yes.

MRS. LAWRENCE. A doctor who delivers babies – at least, where *I* come from... we call them "obstetricians."

MOTHER. (*disturbed*) We also call them obstetricians here, lady.

MRS. LAWRENCE. So, how can that be?

MOTHER. Very simply... Doctor Sanchez is a great family doctor, *and* he also delivers babies.

MRS. LAWRENCE. But does he know how to take care of "geriatrics?"

MOTHER. (*still disturbed*) If you're asking if he has the patience to deal with *senior citizens*, the answer is *yes*.

MRS. LAWRENCE. Do you know any "seniors" who come here?

MOTHER. I bring both my mom and dad here. (*shakes head in disbelief as she turns away*)

MRS. LAWRENCE returns to her magazine and the MOTHER returns to talking to her son.

After a few minutes, MR. LAWRENCE returns to the reception window and hands over the paperwork. The RECEPTIONIST hangs up the phone again and looks over the paperwork.

RECEPTIONIST. Can I take a look at your insurance card?

MR. LAWRENCE. Insurance? I thought Medicare takes care of this...

RECEPTIONIST. Well, yes. But I also need to get a copy of your insurance. You know, with Obamacare and all...

MR. LAWRENCE. We don't have it. We just have Medicare.

RECEPTIONIST. That's fine. (*turns to audience*) But President Obama's not gonna like this.

MR. LAWRENCE. I figure, why pay extra when I've dedicated my whole life to this country? I really think the government *should pay* for this... don't you agree?

RECEPTIONIST. Right – anything you say. (*to audience*) He's been hanging around for too long with his sub-zero wife.

MR. LAWRENCE. What?

RECEPTIONIST. I was asking... are we also gonna see your wife?

MR. LAWRENCE. Why, sure. I filled out both our forms.

MRS. LAWRENCE. (*yells from her seat*) What's taking so long?

MR. LAWRENCE. (*turns to her*) Almost done, sweetie.

MRS. LAWRENCE. Are you flirting with the secretary again? (*yells at RECEPTIONIST*) Is he flirting with you, Miss?

RECEPTIONIST. (*laughs; picks up phone again and dials*) No, ma'am.

MRS. LAWRENCE. (*to audience*) He goes around thinking he's a sexy senior citizen. Ha! I say he's just a dirty old man. (*to boy's MOTHER*) And he had come so highly-recommended...

MOTHER. Who recommended him?

MRS. LAWRENCE. His mother, of course. (*sighs*) Such a nice family, too... You know, he *didn't* use to be like this when we first got married.

MOTHER. Well, I'm sure we all change some as we get older.

MRS. LAWRENCE. (*proudly*) Not me, honey. I've been the same sweetie pie for fifty-eight years of marriage.

MOTHER. Wow, fifty-eight years! (*to audience*) Poor guy.

MRS. LAWRENCE. How long have *you* been married?

MOTHER. I'm... not married. I'm a single parent.

MRS. LAWRENCE. I don't understand you young people these days.

MOTHER. Listen... it wasn't my choice.

MRS. LAWRENCE. (*facetious*) Sure, sure, it's never anyone's fault.

The NURSE opens the reception room door and calls out the name of the next patient. It's the MOTHER and her son's turn. MOTHER gets up in relief and takes her son with her.

MRS. LAWRENCE. (*elbows MR. LAWRENCE, then points to the MOTHER*) Get a load of that...

MR. LAWRENCE. What, sweetie?

MRS. LAWRENCE. That woman who just went in...

MR. LAWRENCE. What about her?

MRS. LAWRENCE. She's not married!

MR. LAWRENCE. That's too bad. Nice looking lady, too.

MRS. LAWRENCE. Will you stop looking at other women! (*hits him*)

MR. LAWRENCE. But, but you're the one that pointed her out to me. (*rubs his arm, where he'd been recently elbowed*) That, I remember.

MRS. LAWRENCE. That doesn't mean you can start fantasizing.

MR. LAWRENCE. I wasn't fantasizing! (*to audience*) At my age, I don't even know what that means.

MRS. LAWRENCE. Oh, shut up you... dirty old man!

MR. LAWRENCE. Yes, sweetie pie. Anything you say.

MRS. LAWRENCE. *Anything* I say? Well then, make yourself useful and go find out what's taking so long.

MR. LAWRENCE. But I just turned in our paperwork.

MRS. LAWRENCE. Are you talking back to me?

MR. LAWRENCE. No sweetie pie, I'm not.

MRS. LAWRENCE. Then go find out! This goddamn knee is killing me! (*hits him again*) You *know* that.

MR. LAWRENCE. Let's calm down.

MRS. LAWRENCE. What?

MR. LAWRENCE. Let's... calm down. You know, so your knee doesn't act up.

MRS. LAWRENCE. I see what you're doing... you're trying to cover up! Boy, you're an idiot! (*to audience*) I married an idiot.

MR. LAWRENCE. Sorry, sweetie.

MRS. LAWRENCE. What are you sorry about now?

MR. LAWRENCE. Nothing, sweetie. Nothing.

MRS. LAWRENCE. So... are you going or what?

MR. LAWRENCE. Yes, I'm going. (*gets up and goes to RECEPTIONIST*) Excuse me? How long do you think it'll be before the doctor sees us?

RECEPTIONIST. (*hangs up phone and responds without thinking*) Do you have an appointment?

MR. LAWRENCE. No, Miss. I just filled out the new patient registrations for me and my wife. Remember?

RECEPTIONIST. Oh yes. Sorry – I was on an important call to... to another doctor's office. (*to audience*) That's right, *another* doctor's office.

MR. LAWRENCE. Are you done with the important phone call?

RECEPTIONIST. Yes, yes. I'm done. (*smiles at audience*)

MR. LAWRENCE. So, when will the doctor see us?

RECEPTIONIST. Well, since you're new patients... and there's two of you...

MR. LAWRENCE. Yes? What are you trying to say?

RECEPTIONIST. You'll be taken in as walk-ins. (*to audience*) That's someone who didn't have an appointment.

MR. LAWRENCE. Okay, now that we understand the terminology... when will we be seen?

RECEPTIONIST. You'll be worked in in-between those patients with appointments. (*looks at watch*) It may be another hour, I think.

MR. LAWRENCE. An hour? Did you say an hour, as in sixty minutes?

RECEPTIONIST. Yes... or longer. The doctor is very busy.

MR. LAWRENCE. (*to himself*) Wanda's not gonna like this... (*goes back to his seat*)

MRS. LAWRENCE. Were you flirting again?

MR. LAWRENCE. (*preoccupied*) Yes...

MRS. LAWRENCE. What?

MR. LAWRENCE. I mean, no sweetie. I was finding out how long before we get seen.

MRS. LAWRENCE. Well? Out with it!

MR. LAWRENCE. It's not good.

MRS. LAWRENCE. (*louder*) Out with it, I say!

MR. LAWRENCE. Alright... (*takes a deep breath*) She says... (*rushes the next part*) it may be an hour or longer. (*holds hands up as if to protect himself from another strike*)

MRS. LAWRENCE. (*doesn't hit him*) What? You're shittin' me, right?

MR. LAWRENCE. Now, you know I would *never* do that on you... sweetie pie. (*to audience*) That's not a nice thing to do.

MRS. LAWRENCE. That's ridiculous! (*gets up*) Let's get outta here, c'mon.

MR. LAWRENCE. Now, now. Let's not be so rash.

MRS. LAWRENCE. What? Now you have a rash?

MR. LAWRENCE. No sweetie... I'm talking about not leaving.

MRS. LAWRENCE. You *know* this knee is killing me! I can't wait that long... I'll be dead by the time it's our turn. And if I'm dead... well shit, I don't need my knee fixed, now do I?

MR. LAWRENCE. You're exaggerating. Just take a deep breath and sit down. You're making a scene.

MRS. LAWRENCE. (*strikes his seat with her cane*) You think I'm making a scene? I'll *show* you a scene...

MR. LAWRENCE. No, no, that's okay. Now, please sit down. I have a good feeling about this place. I *know* the doctor's going to help us... I just know it. Let's stay... please?

MRS. LAWRENCE. Well... all right. (*sits*) But just because you asked me nice.

MRS. LAWRENCE continues to argue toward MR. LAWRENCE. He just nods once in a while and takes all her abuse as time passes by.

The NURSE opens the reception room door and calls the next patients.

NURSE. Lawrence! Eric and Wanda Lawrence!

MR. LAWRENCE gets up fast and attempts to help MRS. LAWRENCE to her feet. She gives him a few slaps on his hands to mean she can fend for herself. They walk toward the NURSE.

Scene 2

The Nurse's station is equipped with the usual – an industrial size adult scale for measuring weights and heights, a pediatric scale for infants, an electronic thermometer, an electronic blood pressure sphygmomanometer with pulse read-out, a Snellen eye chart, and miscellaneous items for blood and laboratory testing.

The classical music is also heard in this area.

NURSE. Hello! How are you today?

MRS. LAWRENCE. Can't you see? I'm dying here.

MR. LAWRENCE. You're not dying. (*turns to NURSE*) She's exaggerating.

NURSE. I see... You hurt yourself?

MRS. LAWRENCE. Yes, I'm hurt. And no, I wouldn't be here if I was feeling fine, now would I?

MR. LAWRENCE. She's having a rough day.

NURSE. She sure is, honey.

MRS. LAWRENCE. So far, just about the only good thing around here is that music.

NURSE. Yes. Doctor Sanchez likes classical music, plus he says it *calms* patients down.

MRS. LAWRENCE. Well, don't just stand there... put us in a room or something.

NURSE. (*to audience*) But then again, I don't think he had *her* in mind.

MRS. LAWRENCE. What's up with your mind? Speak up, I can't hear you very well.

NURSE. I said… (*louder*) … never mind! Why don't we start over again, shall we? (*smiles*) My name's Maggie. How are you today?

MR. LAWRENCE. Hi Maggie. I'm Mr. Lawrence and this is…

NURSE. Don't tell me. This is your *lovely* wife, right?

MRS. LAWRENCE. Enough already! And you – (*to him*) – stop flirting with the nurse!

NURSE. How about if you go first, ma'am? (*points her toward the scale*)

MR. LAWRENCE. That's right – ladies first.

MRS. LAWRENCE. Oh no you don't! I'm not getting on that thing.

NURSE. Why not?

MRS. LAWRENCE. The scales in doctor's offices lie! (*to audience*) Last doctor I saw had a scale that gave me a piece of paper that said, "One at a time, please!"

MR. LAWRENCE. No it didn't. Besides, sweetie, you look fine to me.

MRS. LAWRENCE. You shut up, old man. No one's talking to you.

NURSE. Mrs. Lawrence, we must get your weight. If we don't, the doctor will not like it… and then I may be looking for a new job.

MR. LAWRENCE. Help Maggie out, will ya? C'mon, we don't want her to get fired...

MRS. LAWRENCE. What – are you on her side now?

MR. LAWRENCE. No sweetie. Let's do this, please? (*puts hands together as in prayer, begging*)

MRS. LAWRENCE. Oh, all right already. (*to audience*) I hate it when he does that. (*to him*) Well, just look the other way old man. I don't need you snooping around where you have no business.

MR. LAWRENCE. Oh, c'mon sweetie... how much you weigh (*puts out hands to show large size*) or don't weigh is no big deal.

MRS. LAWRENCE. Well then, if it's no big deal it should be easy for you to look the other way, right?

MR. LAWRENCE. All right, all right. (*looks the other way*)

MRS. LAWRENCE. (*to audience*) I don't need him knowing anything more than he should.

NURSE. You know? I agree with you... I think every woman is entitled to keep two things to herself – her age and her weight.

MRS. LAWRENCE. (*impressed*) Well I'll be... I'm speechless.

NURSE. And I promise I won't say your weight out loud. Would that make you feel better?

MRS. LAWRENCE. Somewhat... (*reluctantly, gets on the scale*)

The NURSE weighs her, then writes it down on the paper chart. The electronic medical records were still having glitches throughout the nation, so this clinic still used paper charts.

MRS. LAWRENCE. Oh, you lie! You lying machine! (*gets off angry; slaps him on the shoulder*) See? I told you these things lie. (*looks for the medicine bag and doesn't find it*) – Don't tell me you forgot the bag again!

MR. LAWRENCE. (*looks around*) Oops! I'll be right back... (*starts to go, then turns*) Maggie, I forgot the bag with our medicines in the lobby.

NURSE. That's quite all right, honey. I'll be right here when you get back.

MRS. LAWRENCE. What a waste. (*to audience*) You know? I married an idiot.

NURSE. Mr. Lawrence seems nice.

MRS. LAWRENCE. You said it – he *seems* nice, but appearances aren't everything. You need more... you need *personality*. (*strikes a pose*)

NURSE. And you're the one with the personality, right?

MRS. LAWRENCE. Are you mocking me, Mollie?

NURSE. Maggie.

MRS. LAWRENCE. What?

NURSE. The name's Maggie.

MRS. LAWRENCE. Yeah – whatever.

NURSE. You know, you should really lay off Mr. Lawrence. Give him some breathing room.

MRS. LAWRENCE. What's that? Breathing? Yeah, he's having some trouble breathing lately. Wait a minute... did he already tell you that? The big flirt!

NURSE. Actually... no. He hasn't said anything. But thanks for letting me know. I'll write it in his chart. (*writes it down*)

MRS. LAWRENCE. Well, I still think he was flirting with you, Mollie.

The NURSE begins to correct her, but chooses not to. MR. LAWRENCE returns with bag in hand. He's puffing a bit.

NURSE. Are you okay, Mr. Lawrence?

MR. LAWRENCE. Yes, Maggie. Why are you asking?

NURSE. Mrs. Lawrence told me you've been feeling short-winded lately?

MR. LAWRENCE. (*moans*) Aghhh – she likes to exaggerate.

NURSE. So, it's not true then?

MRS. LAWRENCE. Go ahead – (*mocks the NURSE*) "Mr. Lawrence," tell the nurse you can't breathe right when you have to do something around the house.

MR. LAWRENCE. You mean, like when I have to mow the lawn?

MRS. LAWRENCE. How convenient, that's what I say!

NURSE. Is that so, Mr. Lawrence?

MR. LAWRENCE. I suppose...

NURSE. That's okay, Mr. Lawrence. You don't have to be brave here. Doctor Sanchez will take good care of you... (*looks at her and decides to add*) ... "both."

MRS. LAWRENCE. He better. We've heard some horror stories about doctors in this part of the country.

NURSE. What do you mean "horror stories?"

MR. LAWRENCE. We've heard doctors get sued a lot around here. Is that true, Maggie?

NURSE. Yes, it's true...

MRS. LAWRENCE. Aha! I knew it!

NURSE. ... but not because of anything doctors do. It's the plaintiff's attorneys – they're chasing down ambulances, handing out their business cards.

MRS. LAWRENCE. Well, I'm still gonna keep an eye on this doctor. Now, can we get on with this?

NURSE. Sure, we're getting there.

MRS. LAWRENCE. Y'know something? My knee is not getting any better just farting around here. Is the doctor *ever* gonna see us?

NURSE. Of course, he is. I just need to take your vitals. It'll only be a minute.

MR. LAWRENCE. You're gonna weigh *me* too?

NURSE. Sure. All our patients get weighed. Why do you ask?

MR. LAWRENCE. Because I already know how much I weigh... (*proudly*) one-fifty five. That's been my weight ever since I was on the University of Minnesota wrestling team. (*shows his bicep*)

MRS. LAWRENCE. Will you stop talking to her and let her *do* her job? (*facetious*) Maybe the doctor will actually *see us* today if you stop flirting with the nurse!

NURSE. (*ignores her*) Thanks for telling me your weight... but I still need to weigh you. (*smiles*) Sorry, doctor's orders.

The NURSE resumes taking and documenting MRS. LAWRENCE's vital signs.

MR. LAWRENCE. Take your time. I've always been fascinated by the doo-hickey there. (*points to the stethoscope around her neck*)

NURSE. Oh, this? (*grabs it*) Nah, this one's a cheapie. Now, the doctor has a really nice one. (*gets idea*) Hey, if you two behave maybe he can show you how to use it!

MRS. LAWRENCE. Enough of the small talk! I'm dying here! You have no idea!

The NURSE proceeds with MR. LAWRENCE's vital signs and gets a surprise when she takes his blood pressure.

NURSE. My, oh my.

MRS. LAWRENCE. What are you mumbling?

NURSE. It's just that Mr. Lawrence's blood pressure is a bit on the high side.

MRS. LAWRENCE. Well, it's supposed to be high... he has *high blood pressure*!

MR. LAWRENCE. How high is it, Maggie?

NURSE. One-eighty over one-ten.

MRS. LAWRENCE. Hey, that's pretty high… even for an old fart like you. (*to audience*) Well, isn't it?

NURSE. (*turns to him*) Are you having any chest pains, Mr. Lawrence?

MR. LAWRENCE. Chest pain? No.

NURSE. Good… and when did you first notice you were having trouble breathing?

MR. LAWRENCE. The other day. I was out in the yard.

NURSE. And what happened?

MR. LAWRENCE. I couldn't finish the entire project.

MRS. LAWRENCE. Project? Ha! (*to audience*) It's just a tiny yard – nothing like what we have back home. Now *that's* a yard.

NURSE. What exactly do you mean, Mr. Lawrence?

MR. LAWRENCE. I couldn't walk more than a few yards without needin' to stop for air.

MRS. LAWRENCE. Did you say "yards?" Why, I really should get a yard stick and smack you over the head with it…

NURSE. (*stern*) Mrs. Lawrence, can you please let him finish. This is important.

MRS. LAWRENCE. Excuse me? And my *knee* is not important?

MR. LAWRENCE. She's right, Maggie. She twisted that knee something awful. I was there.

MRS. LAWRENCE. There you go. (*turns to him*) And *thank you* for finally speaking up for the dying.

MR. LAWRENCE. And then, again… (*Cont'd*)

NURSE and MRS. LAWRENCE turn to pay attention to MR. LAWRENCE.

MR. LAWRENCE. (*Cont'd*) There was another time – at the country club.

MRS. LAWRENCE. (*pleads to nurse*) You're gonna go on with this? Don't forget my knee…

NURSE. Your wife is right, Mr. Lawrence. It's probably best if I take you both to an examination room now. Exam Room 2 is our biggest room and it's available…

MRS. LAWRENCE. (*to audience*) Well Hallelujah!

NURSE. No offense, Mrs. Lawrence, but we're going to Exam Room 2 mainly because of your husband's symptoms… not your knee.

MRS. LAWRENCE. I knew it! (*slaps him on the shoulder*) See, I told you they weren't gonna believe my critical condition…

NURSE. Oh, I believe that you're in pain… don't get me wrong. But you see… Doctor Sanchez has a strict policy that we should take our patients into Exam Room 2 immediately if we suspect an emergency – it's got more room.

MRS. LAWRENCE. Oh, and *he* qualifies as an emergency?

NURSE. That's right.

MRS. LAWRENCE. And my knee? What about my knee? (*begins to writhe in pain*)

NURSE. Oh, get over it, lady... and follow me, both of you. (*walks to the exam room*)

MR. LAWRENCE is about to follow, but MRS. LAWRENCE hits him and forces him to wait for her, and to follow after her. She exaggerates her limp.

Scene 3

Exam Room 2 is your typical examination room, only bigger – it has an exam table, a guest chair, the doctor's stool, a goose-neck lamp, and a built-in desk for writing on the chart. On the wall, there are various charts depicting different anatomical areas of the human body. Mounted on the wall next to the exam table is another sphygmomanometer, plus an oto-ophthalmoscope (for examining the eyes, ears, nose and throat).

The NURSE enters, followed by MRS. LAWRENCE and finally MR. LAWRENCE. She directs them to their seats; sitting MR. LAWRENCE on the exam table, and MRS. LAWRENCE on the chair. She begins to take MR. LAWRENCE's blood pressure once again.

NURSE. I need to repeat your BP... just to make sure. (*inserts earpieces of her stethoscope into her ears*)

MRS. LAWRENCE. (*astonished*) You're serious?

NURSE. (*applies the cuff to his arm; turns toward her*) Excuse me?

MRS. LAWRENCE. I said, you're serious about taking the old fart before me?

NURSE. His condition is more critical, Mrs. Lawrence. (*continues taking the BP*)

MRS. LAWRENCE. Why, I've never been so insulted...

The NURSE shushes her while she's trying to listen for the blood pressure.

MRS. LAWRENCE. Did you just shush me? Where's your damned manners?

The NURSE continues to do her job, ignoring MRS. LAWRENCE.

MRS. LAWRENCE. I'm gonna report you to the doctor. What's his name again?

The NURSE finishes and removes the stethoscope earpieces from her ears. She looks at MRS. LAWRENCE and speaks.

NURSE. You're lucky he's better now. His BP has come down to one-seventy-five over one-o-five.

MRS. LAWRENCE. See? I told you he was alright.

NURSE. No. Actually, he's still very ill... and I'm gonna tell Doctor Sanchez right away. (*starts to leave*)

MR. LAWRENCE. Maggie... (*Cont'd*)

She stops.

MR. LAWRENCE. (*Cont'd*) ... I really don't feel bad.

NURSE. You may not *feel* bad, but trust me, I've seen this before.

MR. LAWRENCE. Well, I guess you know what you're doing.

NURSE. Good. (*she leaves quickly*)

MR. LAWRENCE. (*to audience*) I guess what I was trying to say is that I don't feel bad when I'm resting...

MRS. LAWRENCE. (*to audience*) And I, on the other hand, feel bad even when I'm resting! (*to him*) So, are you happy now?

MR. LAWRENCE. What do you mean?

MRS. LAWRENCE. You know darn well what I mean, old man!

MR. LAWRENCE. Well, I was trying not to say anything...

MRS. LAWRENCE. Ahhh, but you did, you did!

MR. LAWRENCE. It's 'cause... well, she's a smart nurse, sweetie. I tell you.

MRS. LAWRENCE. Just as I suspected... you like her, don't you?

MR. LAWRENCE. Well, yeah... but not that way.

MRS. LAWRENCE. You better watch it, mister.

MR. LAWRENCE. You know you're the only one...

MRS. LAWRENCE. Oh, stop that already!

MR. LAWRENCE. Well, it's true.

MRS. LAWRENCE. You simply weren't gonna be satisfied until you got your way, right?

MR. LAWRENCE. I didn't ask to get my way.

MRS. LAWRENCE. So what happened to all the love?

MR. LAWRENCE. You know that I love you, sweetie pie. (*to audience*) I really love her.

MRS. LAWRENCE. Well, if you really love me then you'd let me go first.

MR. LAWRENCE. Sure, I'll tell the doctor to see you first... okay?

MRS. LAWRENCE. And what are you still doing up there on that table?

MR. LAWRENCE. Oops… sorry, sweetie. (*gets down*)

MRS. LAWRENCE. That's better. (*effortlessly, she jumps and lands on the table*)

The NURSE returns and heads to the exam table, but is surprised to find MRS. LAWRENCE there. She has a pill in her hand and redirects herself toward MR. LAWRENCE.

NURSE. What are you doing sitting here? Didn't I have you on the exam table?

MRS. LAWRENCE. We've decided that I should go first. After all, I'm the one that's hurting.

NURSE. Is that so, Mr. Lawrence?

MR. LAWRENCE. Yes, Maggie. My wife is really hurt… I saw her twist her knee!

NURSE. I know. You already said that. (*shrugs shoulders*) Oh well, here you go… open up and let this sit under your tongue. (*goes for his mouth, but is stopped by him*)

MR. LAWRENCE. What is it?

NURSE. Procardia… a blood pressure medicine.

MRS. LAWRENCE. No, wait a minute. He's not on that one. He's on… oh, what's the name of that pill you take?

MR. LAWRENCE. It's a white one.

NURSE. It doesn't matter if it's a white one or a blue one… or that he doesn't *normally* take this medicine. This is what the doctor wants him to take *right now*.

MR. LAWRENCE. And do I swallow it?

NURSE. No, just leave it under your tongue.

MR. LAWRENCE does as he's told. The NURSE leaves the room once again.

MRS. LAWRENCE. Well, that certainly makes a lot of sense...

MR. LAWRENCE feels he can't talk yet, so he does sign language to ask her 'what?'

MRS. LAWRENCE. You're already getting your treatment, and I'm up here... still waiting. (*looks around in disgust*) Shit! I'm gonna die in this room.

The NURSE re-enters and takes MR. LAWRENCE's blood pressure once again. This time she smiles.

NURSE. Oh, the doctor will be with you shortly, Mrs. Lawrence. Just stay up there and don't move.

MR. LAWRENCE. So, what was the pressure now?

NURSE. It's textbook perfect... one-twenty over eighty.

MR. LAWRENCE. Wow! The medicine works that fast?

NURSE. Yup... another life saved.

MRS. LAWRENCE. And how about this life over here? I'm not gonna make it...

NURSE. Oh, I have a feeling you are going to make it, Mrs. Lawrence.

MR. LAWRENCE. You know what, sweetie?

MRS. LAWRENCE. What now?

MR. LAWRENCE. (*surprised*) I'm actually starting to feel... better.

MRS. LAWRENCE. Oh, come on now... I was born at night, but not *last* night! You, of all people, should know that.

NURSE. No, he's right – this medicine *does* work that fast, usually.

MRS. LAWRENCE. Well, if you asked me, I'd say you're shittin' us.

MR. LAWRENCE. Maggie, can you see if the doctor is on his way? You know... Mrs. Lawrence is in real bad shape.

NURSE. Actually, now that we've taken care of this little emergency...

MRS. LAWRENCE. What? You have another emergency? You leaving us again?

NURSE. No, Mrs. Lawrence, I'm not leaving... I have some more questions to ask you both before the doctor comes in.

MRS. LAWRENCE. More questions? Haven't you asked enough questions for one day?

MR. LAWRENCE. You probably need to know about this, right? (*lifts bag of medicines*)

NURSE. That's part of it...

MRS. LAWRENCE. Now, we're never gonna be seen! And I'll probably end up dying right here on this exam room table! (*begins to weep*)

NURSE. Oh, for Pete's sake... control yourself, woman!

MR. LAWRENCE. (*gets up*) Sweetie, are you okay?

MRS. LAWRENCE. (*stops weeping suddenly*) You're both in this together, right? (*points at him*) You... you're the instigator.

MR. LAWRENCE. No, I'm not.

MRS. LAWRENCE. You've been trying to get rid of me for a long time, haven't you, old man?

MR. LAWRENCE. No, please... don't say that.

MRS. LAWRENCE. I gave you the best years of my life... and this... this is how you repay me?

NURSE. Mrs. Lawrence!

MRS. LAWRENCE. (*to NURSE*) And you! Is this some sort of delay tactic so you can get rid of me?

NURSE. Delay tactic?

MRS. LAWRENCE. Yeah, I can read too, you know.

NURSE. And what, may I ask, have you been reading?

MRS. LAWRENCE. I've read how doctors and nurses enjoy seeing people like me in pain. (*grabs her knee and moans, then stops suddenly*) Are you enjoying seeing me suffer like this?

NURSE. Mrs. Lawrence, I've just about had it up to here with all your antics!

MR. LAWRENCE. (*to NURSE*) She's usually not like this... It's because she's in a lot of pain. (*to audience*) Can't anyone see that?

NURSE. I'm stepping out of the room. When you've settled down a bit, let me know and I'll return to continue doing my job. (*exits*)

MRS. LAWRENCE. Will you get a load of that?

MR. LAWRENCE. I think Maggie is just real busy, sweetie pie. And she probably had to go take care of another patient.

MRS. LAWRENCE. You're always defending other people. Why can't you ever see things my way?

MR. LAWRENCE. I'm sorry, sweetie.

MRS. LAWRENCE. Oh, stop saying you're sorry, already!

MR. LAWRENCE. Okay, okay. (*gets an idea*) Hey, how 'bout if we try and relax? C'mon, do this with me... (*sits, closes his eyes and takes a deep breath*) Concentrate on the nice music. (*he thinks out loud without realizing it*) They say music will tame even the wildest beast...

MRS. LAWRENCE. What?

MR. LAWRENCE. (*opens eyes*) Ahhh, nothing. Nothing.

MRS. LAWRENCE. Did you just call me an animal?

MR. LAWRENCE. No sweetie... I was just trying to say something so we could relax.

MRS. LAWRENCE. Next time you talk about me that way I'll... I'll... (*fuming*) Uuuuh, I can't think what I'll do to you, but I *will* do something.

MR. LAWRENCE. No, please.

MRS. LAWRENCE. If my mother were alive... (*to audience*) I can't believe he called me a... *beast*, of all things.

MR. LAWRENCE. Let's go back to the music, shall we? (*closes his eyes again; listens for several beats*) Do you think it's Beethoven?

MRS. LAWRENCE. (*keeps eyes closed*) What are you mumbling about now? You know I can't hear worth a darn – especially when my eyes are closed.

MR. LAWRENCE. (*louder*) Beethoven! I said, do you think it's Beethoven?

MRS. LAWRENCE. (*gets startled and opens eyes*) Well, you don't have to yell! (*yells back*) And no, it's not Beethoven, it's Mozart!

MR. LAWRENCE. That's Mozart? I could'a bet money it was Beethoven.

MRS. LAWRENCE. Shut up already! And besides, you don't have any money to be gambling. (*to audience, smiling*) I have it all. (*to him*) Old farts like you don't know classical music if it hit you in the face. (*she takes a swing at him from afar*)

MR. LAWRENCE. Well, I used to be pretty good at "Name That Tune."

MRS. LAWRENCE. What's "Name That Tune" got to do with anything? Jesus! (*to audience*) See? What did I tell you? Is he an idiot or what?

MR. LAWRENCE. Please… don't call me that. You don't mean it, do you?

MRS. LAWRENCE. Well, it depends…

MR. LAWRENCE. It depends…?

MRS. LAWRENCE. It depends on whether you're trying to help me relax or if you're only trying to pick a fight. 'Cause I'll whip you – and you know I will!

MR. LAWRENCE. No sweetie. I'm a peaceful person. No fights for me.

MRS. LAWRENCE. And don't say you're a lover, not a fighter… 'cause that's old, just like you.

MR. LAWRENCE shakes his head and looks down in defeat. Looking at him, MRS. LAWRENCE senses victory, and smiles.

MRS. LAWRENCE. Very well then… it's Mozart, and that's final!

MR. LAWRENCE. Oh… now I hear it. It *is* Mozart! You were right all along.

They both sit quietly for a moment. MR. LAWRENCE enjoys the relaxing effects of the music coming from the speaker system. MRS. LAWRENCE remains with her eyes open, and looks around the room, then at her watch. After a while, no more arguing is heard from their room. FADE TO BLACK.

Scene 4

The NURSE knocks on the door of another exam room. DOCTOR JUAN SANCHEZ, early 40s, comes out. The DOCTOR is wearing a white lab coat over his dress clothes and tie. An expensive-looking stethoscope hangs around his neck. They walk over to the counter at the nurse's station.

DOCTOR. What going on, Maggie?

NURSE. Doctor Sanchez! I'm sorry to disturb you, but it's those new patients again...

DOCTOR. The winter Texans?

NURSE. Yes... well, it's really Mrs. Lawrence. She's still making a big fuss over nothing...

DOCTOR. Tell you what – let me just finish with Carlitos here... (*points to the exam room*) ... then I'll be right over, okay?

NURSE. Okay. But don't take too long...

DOCTOR. I won't, Maggie. I won't.

DOCTOR SANCHEZ goes back into the exam room. The NURSE stays in the nurse's station; she wipes her face and shakes her hands. A few moments later, CARLITOS and his MOTHER exit the room, followed by the DOCTOR.

DOCTOR. So, any questions?

MOTHER. None that I can think of.

DOCTOR. Very well. (*beat*) Ms. Lopez, you can go ahead and wait with Carlitos in the lobby... I'll take your prescriptions to the front as soon as I'm done dictating today's note.

MOTHER. Thank you, Doctor. See you in ten days.

DOCTOR. See you. (*to child*) Bye, Carlitos.

CARLITOS smiles but doesn't say a word. The MOTHER encourages him to speak up.

MOTHER. Say "thank you" to the doctor, mi'jo.

CARLITOS. Thank you, Doctor.

DOCTOR. Hope you feel better.

MOTHER. Oh, and Doctor Sanchez...

DOCTOR. Yes?

MOTHER. Don't let those new patients get to you.

DOCTOR. Oh, you... *know* about them?

MOTHER. Let's just say, we've already met in the lobby...

DOCTOR. Thanks for the advice, Ms. Lopez. And take care of this little one (*rubs child's head*) ... so we don't have to put him in the hospital next time, okay?

MOTHER. You know I always do, Doctor Sanchez.

DOCTOR. I know, Ms. Lopez, I know you do.

The NURSE escorts the MOTHER and child to the lobby. DOCTOR SANCHEZ dictates into a hand-held recorder which he takes from his coat pocket.

DOCTOR. Next patient is Carlitos, correction, Carlos Lopez, L-o-p-e-z. (*Cont'd*)

Stops recorder and flips through chart before going on. Continues to dictate and finishes with...

DOCTOR. (*Cont'd*) The impression is... #1) respiratory distress, #2) acute asthmatic bronchitis, and #3) steroid dependency. The plan is... continue on the present regimen and add Zithromax for five days, plus Nasonex. I have answered all the mother's questions to her satisfaction and the follow-up will be in ten days, or sooner p-r-n.

The DOCTOR turns off the recorder and places it down on the counter. He writes the prescriptions and hands them to the NURSE, who in turn hands him the LAWRENCE's charts and points to their exam room... Exam Room 2. She takes the prescriptions to the front office area. He reviews the charts briefly and walks over to Exam Room 2, where the LAWRENCE's are waiting. He takes a deep breath and does the sign of the cross before knocking.

Scene 5

The DOCTOR enters Exam Room 2 and is surprised to find MR. LAWRENCE sitting quietly in a meditation position, with eyes closed. His eyes open when the door closes behind the DOCTOR. MRS. LAWRENCE looks at her watch when she's sure the DOCTOR is looking at her. She doesn't look happy.

DOCTOR. Good afternoon! Mr. and Mrs. Lawrence? (*Cont'd*)

They nod in agreement.

DOCTOR. (*Cont'd*) I'm Doctor Sanchez... Juan Sanchez. (*shakes their hands*)

MR. LAWRENCE. Afternoon, Doc. I was just trying to relax a bit until it was our turn. You've got some nice music here.

DOCTOR. Oh, you like Beethoven? I'm partial to it myself.

MR. LAWRENCE, surprised, looks at his wife.

MRS. LAWRENCE. (*to husband; points her index finger*) Don't... say anything.

DOCTOR. What don't you want him to say, Mrs. Lawrence?

MRS. LAWRENCE. Nothing, Doctor, nothing at all. (*looks at watch again*) Can we get on with it? I'm already dead here... and decomposing.

DOCTOR. Sure... are you in a hurry?

MR. LAWRENCE. Not at all, Doc. Take your time. I'm feeling better already.

MRS. LAWRENCE. (*gives husband dirty look*) He was talking to me.

DOCTOR. Actually, I was talking to both of you.

MRS. LAWRENCE. (*frustrated*) Ahhh... whatever. You know, if you had taken any longer, we would'a had another emergency right here.

DOCTOR. What are you talking about, Mrs. Lawrence?

MRS. LAWRENCE. I'm talking about me! Can't you see I'm dying here? (*shows her cane*)

MR. LAWRENCE. It's true, Doctor. I was there. I've never seen her in such pain!

DOCTOR. Then, why don't we start with you, Mrs. Lawrence? What seems to be the problem?

MRS. LAWRENCE. Well, *you* tell us. You're the Doctor, aren't you?

DOCTOR. Yes, I suppose I am. But... you've got to give me a little bit of help, don't you think? I left my crystal ball at home today... (*smiles*)

MR. LAWRENCE. (*laughs*) That's funny, Doc!

MRS. LAWRENCE. That's not funny; shut up already! Our doctor, here, needs to answer some questions.

DOCTOR. Oh?

MRS. LAWRENCE. Yes. First, where'd you go to medical school? In the U.S.?

DOCTOR. Yes, in the U.S. Why do you ask?

MRS. LAWRENCE. I've heard many rumors about this area.

DOCTOR. What kind of rumors?

MRS. LAWRENCE. That many doctors here aren't *qualified*... and that they get sued a lot. Probably because they're not qualified, I say.

MR. LAWRENCE. Remember, sweet pea? Maggie told us about the ambulance chasers down here.

MRS. LAWRENCE. Shut your yapper, already! (*smiles inappropriately*) Let the good doctor respond.

DOCTOR. Trust me, Mrs. Lawrence, most of my colleagues in this area are *very well-qualified*. In fact, some of them are even on the faculty of some of the most prestigious medical centers in the country.

MRS. LAWRENCE. Hmmm, that's what *you* say. (*unconcerned*) Anyway, I'm still waiting... you haven't answered my question.

DOCTOR. Very well – I went to medical school at the University of Cincinnati College of Medicine, Class of eighty-five.

MRS. LAWRENCE. Cincinnati? I didn't know they had a medical school there!

MR. LAWRENCE. Me neither.

DOCTOR. Well, they do. And, might I add, it's in the top five per cent in the nation.

MRS. LAWRENCE. And where'd you go to college? (*mocking*) In Cincinnati?

DOCTOR. No, ma'am. I went to Trinity University in San Antonio. You know, the *Harvard* of the South?

MR. LAWRENCE. Wow! I'm impressed.

MRS. LAWRENCE. Oh, shut up old man! It really doesn't take much to impress you, anyway.

The DOCTOR writes something in one of the charts.

DOCTOR. You know, Mrs. Lawrence. I like the team approach. Ever heard of it?

MRS. LAWRENCE. No.

DOCTOR. It's a nice little acronym that stands for "Together Everyone Achieves More."

MRS. LAWRENCE. What in tarnation...?

DOCTOR. You see, Mrs. Lawrence? I look at the doctor-patient relationship as a sort of... well, *team*. We all have to contribute so that our team can win...

MRS. LAWRENCE. Hold it right there... stop, I say! (*slowly*) I will not sit here and listen to this... this shenanigan. My health is not some kid's game, Doctor!

DOCTOR. And the health of *my* patients is no game either. Medicine is my life!

MRS. LAWRENCE. Don't talk back to me... we just met!

DOCTOR. You don't get it, do you?

MRS. LAWRENCE. Well, no.

MR. LAWRENCE. Me neither.

DOCTOR. This, *shenanigan*, as you call it, is simply a concept; a way of understanding my approach for a complete and comprehensive health care of my patients.

MR. LAWRENCE. Oh, I think I get it now.

DOCTOR. Mr. Lawrence, you play golf, right?

MR. LAWRENCE. How did you… know?

DOCTOR. It's easy to see. You're still wearing this morning's golf attire. Am I right?

MR. LAWRENCE. Boy, you're good! (*to audience*) He's good, isn't he?

MRS. LAWRENCE shakes her head in disgust.

DOCTOR. What's your handicap?

MR. LAWRENCE. It's usually about an eight.

DOCTOR. Hey, that's pretty good! I have a sixteen, myself.

MR. LAWRENCE. What days do you play?

DOCTOR. (*looks at watch*) Our tee-time is five-thirty today. It's our weekly sundowner.

MR. LAWRENCE. Wish I could join you…

MRS. LAWRENCE. (*interrupts*) Do you have to go on with this?

DOCTOR. Mrs. Lawrence is right. We need to come back to taking care of you... You having trouble when you're out on the course?

MR. LAWRENCE. Doc, I haven't even been able to finish the front nine!

DOCTOR. Why not?

MR. LAWRENCE. It's getting tougher and tougher to breathe.

MRS. LAWRENCE. Oh no, you don't! I see where you're going with this... you're trying to bump me, aren't you?

DOCTOR. Hold on a second, Mrs. Lawrence. (*reviews MR. LAWRENCE's chart and makes a notation in it; goes to him*) Let me take a quick listen to your heart and lungs... (*Cont'd*)

With his stethoscope, the DOCTOR listens to MR. LAWRENCE's heart and lungs. He has a worried look.

DOCTOR. (*Cont'd*) How long have you been feeling this way, Mr. Lawrence?

MR. LAWRENCE. For a while now, but I'd say... worse the last couple of days.

DOCTOR. Are you having to use more than one pillow at night to sleep?

MR. LAWRENCE. Well, as a matter of fact, yes. How did you...?

DOCTOR. Never mind, Mr. Lawrence. And... do you wake up in the middle of the night to catch your breath?

MR. LAWRENCE. Yes, again!

MRS. LAWRENCE. Oh, please!

DOCTOR. (*ignores her*) Mr. Lawrence, I'd like to get an EKG right away...

MRS. LAWRENCE. And what about me? I'm already up here on the table... (*waves*) Hello?

DOCTOR. I won't forget you, Mrs. Lawrence. I just think your husband needs this test now...

MRS. LAWRENCE. (*to husband*) You! Always looking for attention, aren't you?

DOCTOR. That's right, Mrs. Lawrence. He does need attention – and right away, too.

MR. LAWRENCE. What do you think's wrong, Doc?

DOCTOR. I think you may be in congestive heart failure, Mr. Lawrence.

MRS. LAWRENCE. Speak to us in English, will ya?

DOCTOR. I'll explain everything in due time... but right now, (*to MR. LAWRENCE*) you need an EKG. (*speaks through intercom system*) Maggie?

NURSE. (*VO – Intercom*) Yes, doctor?

DOCTOR. I need an EKG on Mr. Lawrence, stat!

NURSE. (*VO – Intercom*) Be right there.

There's a knock on the door, and the NURSE enters. She escorts MR. LAWRENCE away.

DOCTOR. Okay, Mrs. Lawrence. Now I can take a look at you. In the meantime, my nurse will take your husband to our EKG room. That'll take a few minutes, and then I'll review the results with both of you. (*reviews her chart*) So, how did you hurt your leg?

MRS. LAWRENCE. It's not my leg, it's my damned knee.

DOCTOR. Okay... and it's your *left* knee?

MRS. LAWRENCE. Right.

DOCTOR. Oh, it's your *right* knee.

MRS. LAWRENCE. No, damn it! Left, right, right, left... (*frustrated*) Uuuuh... you had it right the first time. This isn't the military, for cryin' out loud.

DOCTOR. So, it's the *left* side, correct?

MRS. LAWRENCE. Yeah, yeah... correct. (*to audience*) I'm glad we got that *right*.

DOCTOR. You were saying?

MRS. LAWRENCE. Nothing, nothing... do go on.

DOCTOR. Very well. When did you hurt your knee?

MRS. LAWRENCE. Going on two weeks now. I was working on my garden... and I stepped on something.

DOCTOR. So, you twisted it?

MRS. LAWRENCE. I don't know! It all happened so fast... but my idiot of a husband says he saw it go like this. (*demonstrates*)

DOCTOR. Did you fall down?

MRS. LAWRENCE. No! Aren't you paying attention? I just showed you how it happened!

DOCTOR. I realize that, but I'm trying to have a clear picture in my mind...

MRS. LAWRENCE. Well, if you'd let me finish you'd have a *clear* picture.

DOCTOR. Very well, continue.

MRS. LAWRENCE. Now I forgot where I was...

DOCTOR. You had just shown me how your husband says you got hurt.

MRS. LAWRENCE. Oh yes – then the pain started. And ohhh, what pain!

DOCTOR. Did you feel a pop? Or a sensation of giving way?

MRS. LAWRENCE. Will you let me finish my story? You know, for being such an educated person, you sure ask a lot of questions...

DOCTOR. That's my job. I've been *trained* to ask a lot of questions... it's for your own good.

MRS. LAWRENCE. Well, that's just not right.

DOCTOR. I think you'll change your mind once your knee starts feeling better.

MRS. LAWRENCE. That's why I'm here. So, can you fix it?

DOCTOR. (*waves for time*) Time out, time out... Have you seen anybody else for this?

MRS. LAWRENCE. More questions? I thought we were done with that.

DOCTOR. We're almost done... so, did any other doctor check you out? Did you go to the Emergency Room?

MRS. LAWRENCE. I didn't go to the Emergency, but I went to a bone doctor.

DOCTOR. When was that?

MRS. LAWRENCE. Last week.

DOCTOR. And what did this doctor say to you?

MRS. LAWRENCE. He wanted to cut me open! (*weeps*) I got scared...

DOCTOR. Who saw you?

MRS. LAWRENCE. I can't remember his name... all these Spanish names sound the same to me.

DOCTOR. In what city?

MRS. LAWRENCE. Right here... north part of town.

DOCTOR. It didn't happen to be Doctor Hinojosa, did it?

MRS. LAWRENCE. I dunno...

DOCTOR. Can you please try to remember?

MRS. LAWRENCE. (*reluctantly*) Kind'a your height? Looks like a movie star?

DOCTOR. Yes...

MRS. LAWRENCE. I suppose that was him.

DOCTOR. He's an excellent Orthopedic Surgeon. I would go to him if I needed a knee operation.

MRS. LAWRENCE. Well, I didn't like him... that's why I'm here. So, can we do this already?

DOCTOR. Sure... and did he take any x-rays?

MRS. LAWRENCE. Yes, he did everything... everything, that is, except cut me open! And that's because I wouldn't let him.

DOCTOR. And what kind of diagnosis did he give you?

MRS. LAWRENCE. You're not serious, are you? I don't know all the medical words...

DOCTOR. What was it that needed surgery?

MRS. LAWRENCE. I don't know... he said something about a *shock absorber*. And that's when I knew he was a quack.

DOCTOR. He was talking about your meniscus... it's like the shock absorber for the knee.

MRS. LAWRENCE. Well, I just got the impression he was a mechanic or something... and I don't need no mechanic doing surgery on me, now do I?

DOCTOR. Have you noticed your knee swell up?

MRS. LAWRENCE. I don't know, I've got fat knees to begin with anyway... But what do my fat knees have to do with anything?

DOCTOR. It would help us confirm your diagnosis.

There's a knock on the door. The NURSE enters with MR. LAWRENCE. He sits back on his chair and the NURSE hands the EKG report to the DOCTOR. DOCTOR studies it and sighs in relief.

DOCTOR. Great news! It doesn't look like you had a heart attack.

MR. LAWRENCE. Why, I could'a told you that much, Doc. I never had any chest pains.

DOCTOR. That's good, Mr. Lawrence. However, many times, a person may not experience any chest discomforts... and still have a heart attack.

MRS. LAWRENCE. You're shittin' us, right?

DOCTOR. Now, why would I do that?

MRS. LAWRENCE. 'Cause you're trying to hurt us?

DOCTOR. Nonsense.

MR. LAWRENCE. Well, wouldn't it feel like an elephant sitting on my chest? I've talked to people who've had this, you know?

DOCTOR. Not necessarily. There are people, especially diabetics, who have what are known as "silent" heart attacks.

MRS. LAWRENCE. Mr. Lawrence may be old... old and stupid, but he's no diabetic!

DOCTOR. I'm not saying he is.

MR. LAWRENCE. So, if I'm not diabetic and I didn't have a heart attack, then why am I in this *failure*?

MRS. LAWRENCE. That's right. (*to audience*) I wanna hear this...

DOCTOR. The condition is called "congestive heart failure." We always want to ask 'why' did this heart begin to fail? Was there a heart attack we weren't aware of? Has there been long-standing hypertension? Is there a thyroid problem? Etc, etc.

MR. LAWRENCE. The high blood pressure... You *know* I have high blood pressure, right?

DOCTOR. Of course, Mr. Lawrence. Who do you think ordered the medicine under your tongue?

MR. LAWRENCE. Oh, yeah...

MRS. LAWRENCE. Ahhh... Doctor? (*Cont'd*)

The DOCTOR turns to her.

MRS. LAWRENCE. (*Cont'd*) Does it make any difference if he didn't quite... *take* his blood pressure medicines?

DOCTOR. He didn't take his medicine?

The LAWRENCES say in unison...

MR. and MRS. LAWRENCE. No.

DOCTOR. For how long?

MR. LAWRENCE. Three months?

DOCTOR. What...? Why...?

MRS. LAWRENCE. (*waves husband off*) Let me explain... because *I* told him not to.

DOCTOR. Why would you do such a thing?

MRS. LAWRENCE. He's not really sick – he wasn't even feeling bad, or anything.

DOCTOR. Let me tell you... a lot of times, patients with high blood pressure don't feel bad.

MR. LAWRENCE. (*to audience*) That was me, alright.

DOCTOR. And that's why it's known as "the silent killer."

MRS. LAWRENCE. Enough already! So, we were wrong. It's an honest mistake... won't happen again.

MR. LAWRENCE. But I'll be okay, Doctor?

DOCTOR. Well... just don't stop taking your medicine unless the doctor tells you to.

Suddenly, there's an urgent knock on the door. The NURSE opens the door.

NURSE. Doctor Sanchez! Quickly, we need you next door!

The DOCTOR rushes out and leaves the LAWRENCES' charts on the desk. The NURSE follows.

MRS. LAWRENCE. Pssst...

MR. LAWRENCE. Yes, sweetie?

MRS. LAWRENCE. Look over there. (*points toward charts*)

MR. LAWRENCE. Yes, what about 'em?

MRS. LAWRENCE. Our charts are wide open, stupid!

MR. LAWRENCE. (*shocked*) No! I hope you're not thinking what I think you're thinking…

MRS. LAWRENCE. Oh, shut up and get over there!

MR. LAWRENCE gets up and goes to the charts. He looks at the one on top; it's his. He reads what the DOCTOR has written down.

MRS. LAWRENCE. I'm waiting!

MR. LAWRENCE. Oh my God! You're right!

MRS. LAWRENCE. What… what? Speak up!

MR. LAWRENCE. It says here, "S-O-B!"

MRS. LAWRENCE. I knew it! He just wants to go to his golf game… the bastard!

MR. LAWRENCE. But, he seems so nice…

MRS. LAWRENCE. He doesn't care about me… and he doesn't care about *you* either!

MR. LAWRENCE. I… can't believe it.

MRS. LAWRENCE. You see, old man? In his book, you're just an S.O.B.! (*Cont'd*)

MR. LAWRENCE looks down, sadly. He realizes that MRS. LAWRENCE has been right all along.

MRS. LAWRENCE. (*Cont'd*) No wonder they get sued all the time! The sons of bitches...

MR. LAWRENCE. I... believe you, sweetie.

MRS. LAWRENCE. You better, old man.

MR. LAWRENCE hears the door open slightly. The DOCTOR holds it ajar while he finishes giving orders to the NURSE. MR. LAWRENCE has enough time to return to his seat without getting caught. The DOCTOR enters.

DOCTOR. Sorry about that – we have a patient who's gonna need an ambulance.

MRS. LAWRENCE. (*looks at her watch*) The way things are going, we're gonna need one too!

DOCTOR. I really don't think so, Mrs. Lawrence. (*places stethoscope on desk*) Now, let's take a look at your knee.

MRS. LAWRENCE. (*clears throat*) Ahem... before you start...

DOCTOR. Yes, Mrs. Lawrence?

MRS. LAWRENCE. I *need* you to lend your instrument... (*points to the stethoscope*) to Mr. Lawrence.

DOCTOR. Oh? And why, may I ask?

MRS. LAWRENCE. So I can get him off my back! He keeps bugging me that he wants to try it...

MR. LAWRENCE. Doc, do you mind?

DOCTOR. (*smiles*) Go ahead, Mr. Lawrence... just don't hurt yourself.

MR. LAWRENCE. (*goes to get it; puts it on and turns to wife*) May I?

MRS. LAWRENCE. Not now! Can't you see I'm finally gonna get checked?

DOCTOR. That's okay, Mrs. Lawrence... he can take a listen while I examine you.

MRS. LAWRENCE. Alright, then. Knock yourself out, old man. (*sticks out her chest*)

MR. LAWRENCE. (*listens to heart*) Oh, oh...

MRS. LAWRENCE. Now what?

MR. LAWRENCE. I can't hear a thing. Does that mean... (*to audience*) she doesn't have a heart?

MRS. LAWRENCE. (*slaps at him*) Get away from me! Let the doctor work.

The DOCTOR continues to examine MRS. LAWRENCE's knee. He goes over several maneuvers.

MRS. LAWRENCE. Careful, careful!

DOCTOR. Don't worry, Mrs. Lawrence. I'm a professional.

MRS. LAWRENCE. Yeah, but you're *hurting* me!

DOCTOR. I'll be as gentle as I can, trust me. (*Cont'd*)

MR. LAWRENCE is still amused with the stethoscope. He listens to his own heart, then shakes his head. He taps on the bell to check if it's working.

DOCTOR. (*Cont'd*) I do believe you have some fluid in there. The best thing to do is to take it out.

MRS. LAWRENCE. You mean... with a needle?

DOCTOR. Yes... that's how we *usually* take fluid out.

MRS. LAWRENCE. Uuuuh – I hate needles with a passion!

DOCTOR. So, what are we going to do, Mrs. Lawrence?

MRS. LAWRENCE. I guess at this point, I'll do anything... if it'll get rid of the pain.

DOCTOR. Good. (*explains*) What I'm going to do, Mrs. Lawrence, is to insert a needle into your knee. Then I will *aspirate*... (*does a suction motion*) the fluid you have inside.

MRS. LAWRENCE. Do I really have to hear this?

DOCTOR. I'm afraid you do. It's called "informed consent."

MRS. LAWRENCE. Well... just get to the point.

DOCTOR. Actually, this aspiration will be both therapeutic *and* diagnostic.

MRS. LAWRENCE. What the hell...?

DOCTOR. Therapeutic because we're removing a lot of the pressure you have built-up, which causes pain... (*Cont'd*)

MRS. LAWRENCE nods.

DOCTOR. (*Cont'd*) And diagnostic because the appearance of the fluid can help us arrive at a diagnosis.

MRS. LAWRENCE. Well, go ahead and *arrive* over here. (*taps knee*) I'm as ready as I'll ever be. (*to audience*) Should I trust him?

DOCTOR. (*calls over intercom*) Maggie, you there?

NURSE. (*VO – Intercom*) Yes, doctor?

DOCTOR. I need a large bore needle with a sixty c.c. syringe... plus one and one of Xylocaine and Decadron. Got that?

NURSE. (*VO – Intercom*) Sure, doctor. Be right there.

DOCTOR. Thanks.

MRS. LAWRENCE. Is she coming?

DOCTOR. Yes, she'll be here shortly. (*goes to drawer*)

MRS. LAWRENCE. It's about time... Jesus! I don't think I can take any more of this pain! (*grabs knee*)

DOCTOR. (*pulls out some papers from the drawer*) While we're waiting for Maggie to bring everything we need for your knee aspiration, I'd like for you to look at this *Consent Form* and sign it, Mrs. Lawrence. It goes over everything that you can expect related to this procedure. And I can answer any questions you may have at this time.

MRS. LAWRENCE. What? More paperwork?

DOCTOR. It's the standard of care, Mrs. Lawrence.

MRS. LAWRENCE. This is ridiculous! (*waves at the DOCTOR*) Give me your pen, c'mon. (*Cont'd*)

The DOCTOR hands her his pen.

MRS. LAWRENCE. (*Cont'd*) Let's get this over with. (*signs the papers without reading them*)

There is a knock on the door. The NURSE enters with two syringes, a cotton ball, an alcohol swab, and a Band-aid. She hands the items to the DOCTOR. The NURSE leaves, shaking her head after looking at the exaggerating MRS. LAWRENCE.

DOCTOR. Okay, Mrs. Lawrence. This is going to hurt you more than it's going to hurt me.

MRS. LAWRENCE. What?

DOCTOR. Just kidding. You're gonna feel a whole lot better.

MRS. LAWRENCE. (*threatening*) I better...

The DOCTOR cleans the injured knee with the alcohol, then begins to aspirate red fluid. MRS. LAWRENCE reacts violently.

MRS. LAWRENCE. Ouch...! You're hurting me again!

DOCTOR. Calm down, calm down.

MRS. LAWRENCE. Speak up! I can't hear you when you're doing that to me...

DOCTOR. (*louder*) I said, try to calm down, Mrs. Lawrence. We're almost done.

MRS. LAWRENCE. (*starts to hyperventilate*) Oh, you're gonna kill me!

DOCTOR. (*continues with procedure*) No, I'm not... (*finishes and pulls out the needle*)

MRS. LAWRENCE. You sonnafabitch!

MRS. LAWRENCE *suddenly kicks with her bad leg and strikes the* DOCTOR *on the jaw. He stumbles back and lands on top of the sitting MR. LAWRENCE, who was now examining the stethoscope with both hands. He doesn't know what to do with the groggy* DOCTOR *on top of him.*

MRS. LAWRENCE. Get him! Get him, you idiot!

MR. LAWRENCE *obeys, and begins to choke the* DOCTOR *with his own stethoscope. They both get up in a struggle. The* DOCTOR *tries to grasp for air. Beethoven's 5th Symphony is heard; it crescendos along with the action in this scene. MR. LAWRENCE doesn't let go of his grip.*

MRS. LAWRENCE. That's right, you sonnafabitch! You deserve that!

DOCTOR. *(being choked)* Wh... Why?

MRS. LAWRENCE. You wrote on his chart that he's a son of a bitch!

DOCTOR. *(still being choked)* That's... that's not... true...

MRS. LAWRENCE. Oh, don't give us that! We *saw* it with our own eyes... *(points to her eyes)*

DOCTOR. *(gasping for air)* S.O.B. means "short... of... breath."

MR. LAWRENCE *still holds on to the choke. He looks at her and then looks at his choke hold, pleading. The music continues.*

MR. LAWRENCE. Maybe he's telling the truth, sweetie?

MRS. LAWRENCE. *(points at him)* Don't you dare...!

MR. LAWRENCE. But, what if...?

MRS. LAWRENCE. Don't let go! Don't let go!

The DOCTOR takes one last breath and his body falls limp in MR. LAWRENCE's arms. The music comes to a climax. MR. LAWRENCE lets him down and leaves the stethoscope around the DOCTOR's neck.

MR. LAWRENCE. (*shocked*) Is he... dead?

MRS. LAWRENCE. If he is... serves him right! You saw what he was doing to me!

MR. LAWRENCE. But... I didn't want to kill... him.

MRS. LAWRENCE. What are you mumbling now?

The siren of an ambulance is heard closer and closer. There's a lot of commotion outside the room. MRS. LAWRENCE opens the door slightly and peeks outside.

MRS. LAWRENCE. Get our things and let's get outta here! Hurry!

MR. LAWRENCE grabs the bag of medicines and MRS. LAWRENCE gets her cane. Voices are heard outside the LAWRENCE's room.

NURSE. Quickly, the patient's in Exam Room six!

PARAMEDIC. What do we have here?

NURSE. Heart attack!

PARAMEDIC. Let's go, let's go!

The PARAMEDICS and NURSE enter Exam Room 6.

The LAWRENCES leave Exam Room 2 and get lost among the clinic-full of patients and employees trying to see what's happening. Just as the door closes behind the LAWRENCES, the DOCTOR begins to gasp for air. He struggles, but gets to his feet.

When the LAWRENCES reach the lobby, they find it completely empty.

MR. LAWRENCE. C'mon, c'mon!

MRS. LAWRENCE. Don't yell at me! Hey, wait a minute!

MR. LAWRENCE. What, sweetie?

MRS. LAWRENCE. (*astonished*) My knee!

MR. LAWRENCE. Not now! We'll find somebody else to take care of it later!

MRS. LAWRENCE. No, you stupid fool! My knee… it's not hurting anymore! I guess you *were* right about the doctor…

MRS. LAWRENCE throws away the cane in the lobby and it hits a hanging sign. MR. LAWRENCE opens the door for her, and she hits him as she skips away happily. He follows after her.

DOCTOR SANCHEZ stumbles to the lobby, rubbing his throat. He watches as MR. and MRS. LAWRENCE flee the scene. He leans on the reception counter and his attention is drawn to a swinging hanging sign that reads, "Winter Texans Welcome!"

THE END

ABOUT THE AUTHOR

José Luis "Jay-el" Hinojosa, MD and his family emigrated from Mexico to the USA when he was only 7 years old. He was fortunate to attend an Ivy League school (Brown University) for his undergraduate studies, after which he matriculated at the University of Cincinnati College of Medicine (Cincinnati, OH) to earn his Doctor of Medicine degree. After completing his specialty in Family Medicine in south Texas, he had a successful private practice for 25 years.

Today, he is Chief of Staff at Stanton County Hospital and Medical Director at Stanton County Family Practice in Johnson, Kansas. Always wanting to continue learning, he will attain his Masters of Science in Healthcare Administration from Grand Canyon University in early 2016.

Besides being a physician leader, Dr. Hinojosa is also a martial arts leader. He has trained and taught the martial arts for 40 years and has won many titles, including *World Championships* in Germany and México, multiple Hall of Fame awards, including a *Lifetime Achievement Award*, and he is a crowd favorite with his powerful, creative, and highly entertaining routines – most notably, his award winning form entitled *Reflections of an Old Man*, where he dresses up as an elderly man with a cane and dazzles the crowd while reminiscing about his youth. Speaking of youth, Dr. Hinojosa has three children (JL, Laura, and Alexis) who always inspire him; he is also happily married to Maria Elena Hinojosa.

As an innovator, Dr. Hinojosa invented a fascinating medical device (patent pending) that is positioned to revolutionize health care around the globe – please go to **www.TheMDMedical.com** for more information on this. He also invented the popular game *Grand Champion*®, the first ever card game related to the martial arts and it teaches good moral values.

Exam Room 2 marks the 13ᵗʰ book authored by Dr. Hinojosa and his second play. *Exam Room 2* is a work of fiction, although the names of two people who made a positive impact in Dr. Hinojosa's life were used – unlike Mrs. Lawrence from *Exam Room 2*, Ruby Lawrence was a very pleasant, elderly patient for many years with Dr. Hinojosa (she was the "Star of the Month" one time and when she was in her 90s, her birthday was celebrated at Dr. Hinojosa's clinic) and Maggie Morales was a wonderful and dedicated nurse for more than 13 years with Dr. Hinojosa. Yes, this work is in their honor.

Dr. Hinojosa co-wrote the screenplay for an independent feature length film (*Campeón: A Journey of the Heart*). He just finished penning his first book entirely (yes, 100%) in Spanish, entitled *¡El Lenguaje de los Triunfadores!* It is the Spanish version of his highly-popular personal improvement book, *The Language of Winners!* He is currently working on the Spanish version of *Master and Disciple* and cannot wait to release it to his Spanish-speaking family, friends, and followers. For more information on how to get ahold of any of his books, please go to **www.BooksByDrHinojosa.com**

Dr. Hinojosa is a stage actor and has also appeared in several feature-length films. His most recent acting work was in the world premiere run (Nov. 2011 and Jan. 2012 in three south Texas cities) of *Tales of the Hidalgo Pump House*, where he played one of the lead characters, Luis Rivera, and had the opportunity to display his singing, dancing, and comedic timing; in his most recent film, he played the villain in the feature-length 2009 Warrior Pictures film *Campeón: A Journey of the Heart*.

As a professional speaker, Dr. Hinojosa is equally fluent in Spanish as he is in English keynote presentations. He shares his experiences with his audiences with such passion and clarity, that he always "connects." It is no wonder that Dr. José Luis "Jay-el" Hinojosa is highly sought out as a motivational and inspirational speaker not only in the USA, but also in México. He is a specialist in *Leadership and Success* topics, with his most popular keynotes being: *The Making of a Leader, Dream Your Way to Success, The Five Business Lessons to Learn from Breaking Boards, and Develop a World Champion Attitude.*

DID YOU ENJOY THIS BOOK?

- Students, did this book inspire you to want to see it as a live production on stage?

- Teachers, do you think you'd like to produce *Exam Room 2* at your school or in your community? If so, just send me an e-mail at **DrH@TheMDMedical.com** and we can make it happen!

- Would you recommend this book to your friends and loved ones?

If so, show the world that you care and order a copy of *Exam Room 2* for your friends and loved ones right now!

HERE'S HOW TO ORDER

www.BooksByDrHinojosa.com

www.ingramcontent.com/pod-product-compliance
Lightning Source LLC
Chambersburg PA
CBHW020605030426
42337CB00013B/1215